Are you Really Closing your Supply Chain?

My Research my Choice
Forward Supply Chain
Part I

Dr. Rabindranath Bhattacharya

Preface

This book is aimed at an important and underserved niche within supply chain management education and application: closed loop supply chain management where the product travels from cradle to cradle and not to grave. Products get a new life or become hybrid (combination of old and new) as it travels down the forward line to customers and back to the starting point through the reverse line from customers and again back to customers through forward line. All supply chain professionals need to understand this for their own survival in today's competitive world. This book is based on the research work carried out by the author for nearly four years in the Department of Management studies of Indian Institute of

Technology Madras, India and is meant to guide the practitioners (especially original equipment suppliers for auto parts) towards design of models, analysis of the same, drawing insights from them and ultimately providing superior service to customers.

The author with more than thirty-five professional experience in the manufacturing industries around the globe carried out remanufacturing activities in various organizations and was able to save substantial amount of cost by utilizing the used parts/products and recycling raw materials. It was observed that although the reverse supply chain is similar to forward supply chain in the reverse direction the areas of difficulty encountered by the author were mainly acquisition prices of returned products, different quality grades of acquired products, sorting and distribution of materials to stages of repair and reuse of the repaired material/product on the forward supply chain or resale of the same in niche market. Question was how to maximize the integrated operation profitability to get an idea of the optimum values of the decision variables and take corrective actions to operate near the optimum values? This was the motivation behind the research on closed loop supply chain in a remanufacturing scenario for the author.

The author hopes to bring out the entire book in three parts and the first part of the series describes what is supply chain or forward supply chain to be precise, its evolution, motivation behind it, design and structure of the same and the way forward. Reverse supply chain and Closed loop supply chain integrating both forward and reverse chains would be taken up in the remaining two

parts. This book is unlike any text book on Supply

chain and is meant for general public as well as professionals and students who would like to have a general knowledge of the subject without going through complicated theories and problems. The dialogue between colleagues in between hope would help the readers get rid of monotony and a feel of reality.

The author would feel satisfied if this book motivates the numerous original equipment suppliers, who are still not in the business of remanufacturing their own products, to go for the same before their competitors in the unorganized sectors, doing roaring business all over the world, snatch away their bread as well the technology! Risk is high but so is the return.

Time is running out very fast for them! The original equipment suppliers in the twenty first century must not be concerned for *Profit* only bur also for *Planet* and *People* (environment). This would ensure that there is a healthy growth of the company but not at the cost of the Mother Earth inclusive of our environment and society at large.

Dr. Rabindranath Bhattacharya

Kolkata

31/05/2019

Contents

Part I
Forward Supply Chain

Chapter I
Introduction

Mike was always an avid follower of cricket. Although I played cricket during my college days, I was never obsessed with it.

"Robin, come with me to Marriot and let us enjoy the test match between India and England on a big TV"

"Fine, let's go. It's good that you have not asked me to come to Lords. It's a sheer waste of time."

It was a typical English weather with sky little overcast with clouds and raining in driblets. I felt like drenching myself in it like college days but the age has caught me up and I did not venture out. Club was exquisitely decorated with medieval furniture and chandeliers, paintings of Picasso on the wall, a fountain in the middle where a naked woman statue was taking bath in the fountain water, real palm trees on both sides, floor made out of glass and a picturesque green golf ground on the back side visible through the transparent glass. I was lost for a moment.

Game was over and Mike was dejected since England lost by one hundred and odd runs.

"It's a game. Take it easy, Mike" I tried to console him.

"Anyway, Robin, I wanted to find a quiet place to understand about supply chain from you. What's this? Everybody is talking about it. Could you please explain to me in details? You seem to read a lot and have more practical experience and patience than me and I was informed that you are also planning to do go for research on supply chain management after retirement. Excuse me if I have intruded into your private space."

"Mike, do not be so formal. Yes, the information happens to be true. Coming back to the subject, in fact, manufacturing business scenario has been rapidly changing during the last two decades. Customers have become more demanding as you know and require that the suppliers disclose their operation data as much as they desired. The idea behind this is to reduce cost and lead time directly but indirectly they are out to deprive you of the extra profit you expected to earn. The focus today is on creating value through personalized and individualized offerings to customers while at the same time traditional requirement such as high quality and low cost remain important (Krikke, 2003)." I said. Mike, being a finance man, was little impatient. "Robin, could you please explain it with an example from the past?" He asked.

"We get a good insight from examples of food/clothing supply chain of ancient group of people who searched for food or warm clothing. They used proper weapons to kill the animals, remove their hide for covering their bodies and roast the meat for food. This required careful planning and management of the said supply chains.

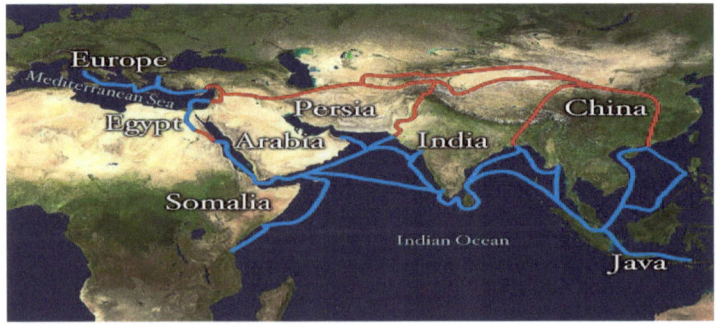

Figure 1.1 Supply chain for spice routes in 1453

Over centuries the supply chain evolved from its primitive state to something what we see today and the chain of links connecting all the suppliers of raw materials to the finished products combined with the logistics started getting longer and complex." I explained, "Figure 1.1 shows the complexity even in the year 1453." "What are the things which added to the complexity in supply chain?" Mike asked.

"Globalization of manufacturing operations as well as advent of information Technology added to the complexity more than anything else. The links of supply chain involved being spread all over the world are hence difficult to manage as individual components. It was in 1980s that the companies started realizing the benefit of the cooperation with the suppliers outside their organization (Turner, 2012). To optimize the entire supply network, companies must actively involve in the other links of the chain (Lummus and Vokura, 2003). This is necessary to manage the operations seamlessly across the globe and meet the varying demands of the customers in the most efficient manner. The concept/movement referred to as supply chain management (SCM) was thus born to ensure smooth flow of materials along the chain." I said, "Figure 1.2 shows the schematic diagram of a Globally dispersed supply chain of a dress manufacturer in Hongkong receiving orders from and shipping Jackets to US based company.

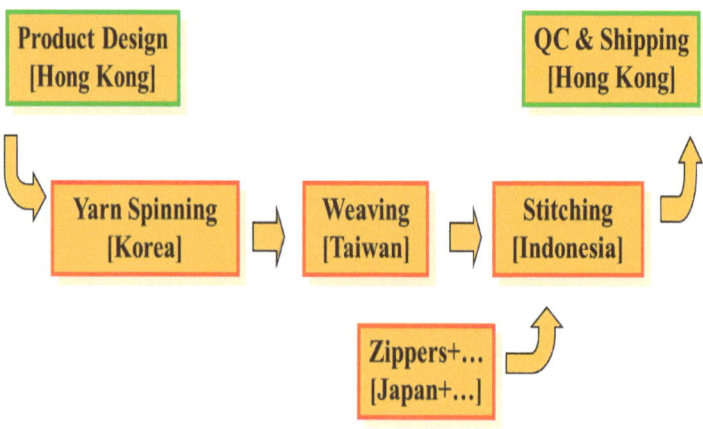

Figure 1.2 Globally dispersed supply chain

"Robin, this seems to be very risky from the disruption point of view. By the how did you avoid disruption of the supply chain when the steel prices went through the roof few years back in India?" Mike was sipping beer from a big mug.

"I did not keep quiet when everybody was complacent. I knew the supply from Indian company would stop since I could not afford to accede to their demand for phenomenal price rise. I went to China and Japan to develop alternate sources for my steel requirements much before others and I was able to switch sources before the impending disaster. Although it was a delicate situation but I had to manage it successfully to protect the bottom line. I shifted the steady demand products to far off suppliers and managed not so steady demand from Indian supplier." I spoke with confidence.

"Great. But Robin, do you feel that information technology changed the whole picture during the last decade of the twentieth century?"

"You are right Mike. It helped a lot. This movement was further accelerated and refined by the advent of Japanese concept of production and quality during 1980s and innovation in communication like internet, e-commerce, and software and computer technology during 1990s. Sharing of information and planning with upstream or downstream entities in and outside the organizations became easy and companies started managing the links better (improving performance) and started coming closer to the customers by giving better services and quality. Collaborative planning CP (Dudek and Stadtler, 2005), Efficient consumer response (ECR)

(Corsten and Kumar, 2005), vendor managed inventory (VMI) (Dong and Xu, 2002), supplier relationship management (SRM) (Lamming, 2005), customer relationship management (CRM), internal supply chain management system, operation research (OR) techniques in network design and distribution are few of the concepts/tools implemented to actually realize the benefit of SCM. Many of the firms have supply chain management as a major tool for competitive excellence. In the recent years, as an effective business philosophy, supply chain management, has gained tremendous amount of attention from both academicians and practitioners (Chan and Qi, 2003). It can be clearly observed from the literature that a large number of firms have begun to look beyond their own organizational boundaries to consider the overall design of their supply chains for improved performance. Lambert *et al.* (1998) highlighted that the supply chain business processes comprise of customer relationship management, customer service management, demand management, order fulfillment management, manufacturing flow management, supplier relationship management, product development and commercialization and Returns Management." I replied and projected the Figure 1.3 for reference on the screen.

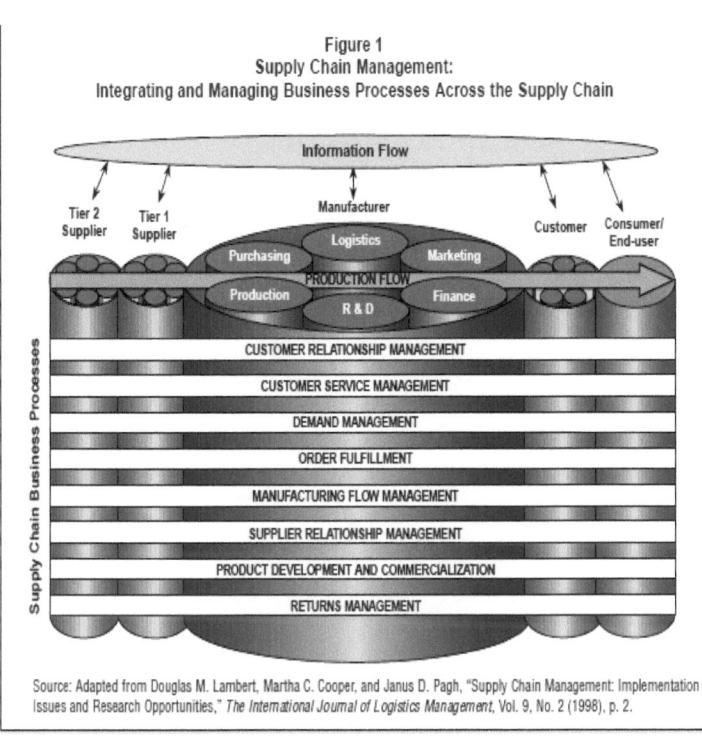

Figure 1
Supply Chain Management:
Integrating and Managing Business Processes Across the Supply Chain

Source: Adapted from Douglas M. Lambert, Martha C. Cooper, and Janus D. Pagh, "Supply Chain Management: Implementation Issues and Research Opportunities," *The International Journal of Logistics Management*, Vol. 9, No. 2 (1998), p. 2.

Figure 1.3 Entities and integration of supply chain

Mike was little bit excited but shot another question at me - "How the organizations would take care of the risks involved in building up right kind of supply chain when the operations are spread across the globe?"

"To compete successfully, in today's market environment, firms need to simultaneously manage the activities of purchasing, design, manufacturing, distribution and services to the customers in an efficient and effective manner inclusive of returns management or reverse supply chain. Network and Distribution have become very complex vide Figures 1.4, 1.5, 1.6 and 1.7

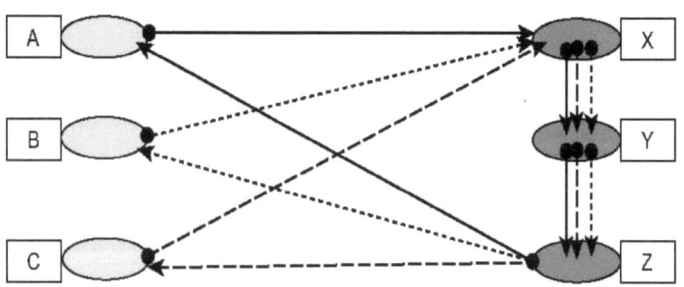

Figure 1.4 Milk run system of distribution

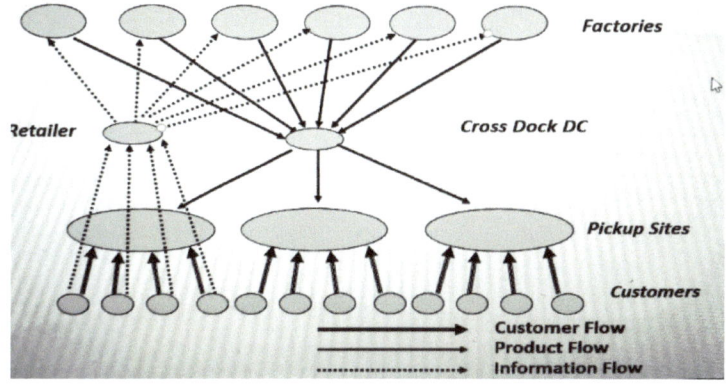

Figure 1.5 Customer pick up with distributor/customer

storage

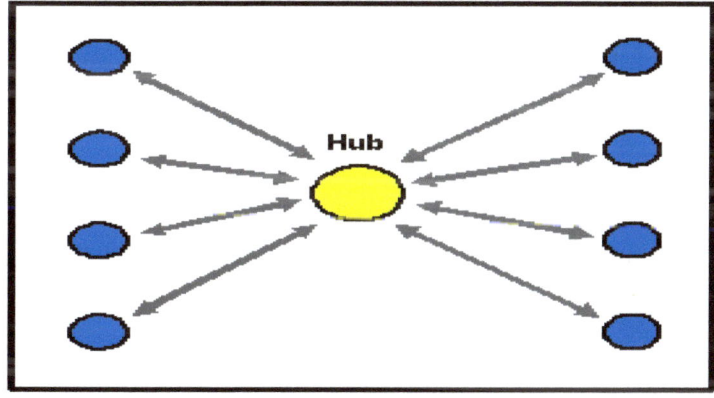

Figure 1.6 Hub and spoke delivery

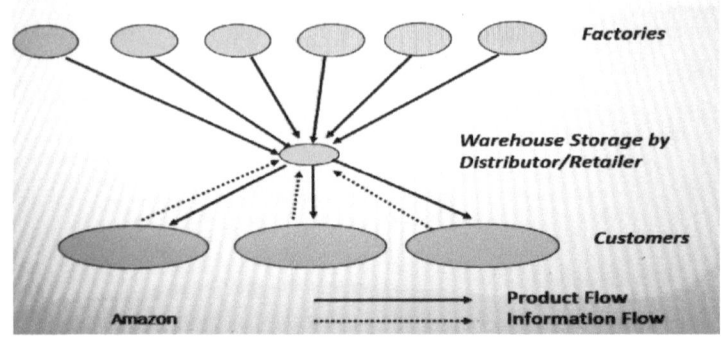

Figure 1.7 Distributor storage with carrier delivery

Hence, effective management of the supply chain requires perfect integration of the internal and external operations of channel members in the chain. And to integrate various entities you need to collect data and analyze. For example, your forecast and actual demand of the products or your demand and actual supply or demand and supply from suppliers never match. Question is how to minimize the error in each case so that

26

your supply chain efficiency increases and your inventory level comes down."

"But, how to handle the enormous amount of data we are collecting every day. It seems eighty percent of these are useless and junk" Mike asked.

"That is where you would have to correct yourself. Data is never useless. They are to be nurtured and be used to our advantage. For your information Amazon probably was the first in the field to suggest some books for future purchase based on your pattern of purchase in the past. They are using data with analytics and that is why they are successful. I think you have noticed this in your Kindle."

"Oh, yes."

"That is what is required. You would have to be proactive instead of reactive. You would have to build up an organization where decisions are taken based on facts and data. Your executives are to be equipped with the necessary tools and techniques accordingly. Availability of data and the analytical tools both are required to build up an efficient supply chain. Radio tags, memory chips, Internet of things, 3-D printing and so on are not the things for future but are a reality. Hence to reap the benefit of big data analytics companies must work along the entire supply chain and optimize the system or find the most satisfying solution. Big data analytics can make that happen.

"Robin, you have made the things very clear, but I would appreciate if you organize an hour presentation in our Chicago unit for all of our colleagues one day covering aspects like definition and structure of the supply chain, its evolution, motivation and its journey towards reverse supply chain. And with Chairman's presence things are likely to move much faster."

"OK, no problem. Come to the conference room next Wednesday positively. Let all the staffs starting from Manager to Chairman be present. It would be easy for me to explain the things in one forum. I reiterate that supply chain management can no longer be neglected, if you really want to grow." I confidently uttered.

"Robin, let's call it a day. It's time for dinner. Do not worry I would inform our Chairman, Dr. Guttenberg." Mike stood up

"Let me also go to my room, change my dress and come back for dinner." I was also damn tired.

****

Chapter II
Evolution

Building a strong supply chain is essential for business success. But when it comes to improving their supply chains, few companies take the right approach (Lee *et al.*, 2006). In fact, supply chain management started with logistics management initially. However, the evolution of supply chain management inclusive of logistics management took place broadly in three stages as described below.

- Functional management (1960-1970) – Functions/department such as purchasing, shipping, and distribution are each managed separately. This means these departments in an organization were working in silos and there was hardly any coordination or integration.

- Internal integration (1980s) – The management of the supply chain functions of a single facility understood the importance of integration and were more unified and started functioning as a team headed by a single individual

- External integration (1990s) – the management of supply chain functions throughout the chain as a team ensuring cooperation and coordination with external agents like suppliers and customers as well.

Evolution of supply chain both at company level and process level are shown in Figures 2.1 and 2.2.

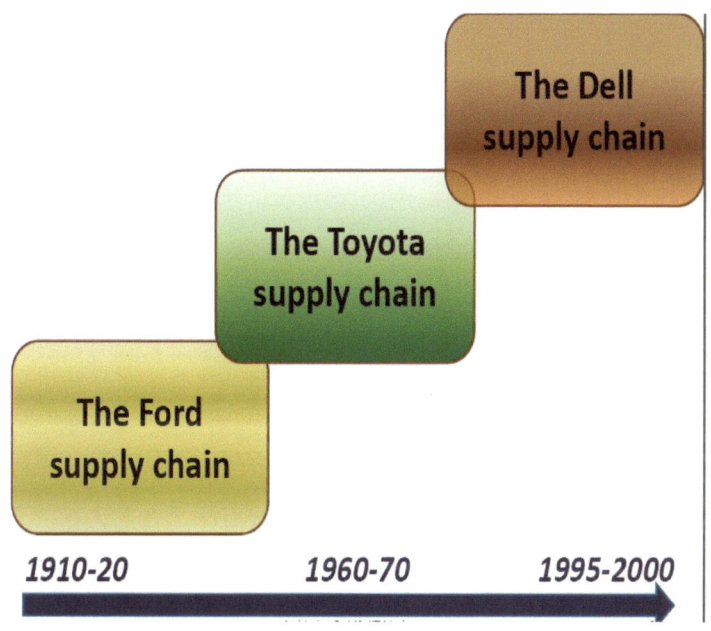

Figure 2.1 Broad Evolution of Supply chain in the Western World

The Ford supply chain was originally the first mass producing industry in the world. But the company was producing even their own steel for the manufacture of passenger cars, a phenomenon quite unthinkable at present.

Toyota supply chain changed the concept and ensured that all critical items like engine and gear box would be made inside the company and the rest of the products would be procured from suppliers. Dell revolutionized the concept and procured everything from vendors reducing the cost of inventory beyond imagination. That was the reason why the inventory turnover figure once reached a figure of sixty which means they have any time six days (360/60) inventory in their system anytime. In industries manufacturing auto components, we could hardly touch twenty-five in India.

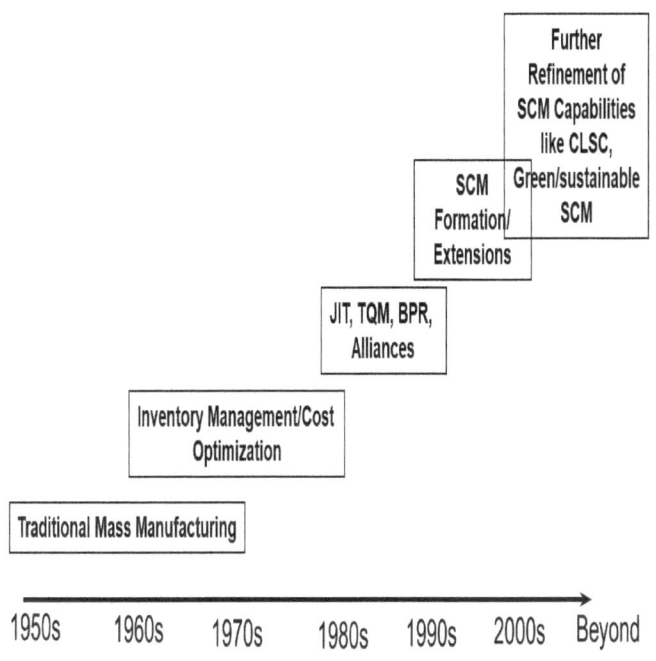

Figure 2.2 Evolution of supply chain at process level

As per Chopra *et al.* (2007) supply chain Management (SCM) represents confluence of four streams of knowledge and practices which were being followed by industries till seventies in developed as well as developing countries. These were purchase management, materials

35

management, logistics and distribution. Job of purchase people ended with the procurement of materials from suppliers at the lowest possible prices and handing over the same to production planning and control (PPC). PPC took control of materials/products once these were cleared by incoming inspection department. Manufacturing was being carried out by production department as per the guidelines given by PPC. Major purchase decisions were being taken by the owners or their relatives and hence economic buying was always a strategic responsibility (Spieler and Murray, 2008). PPC would ensure that these materials along with parts produced inside the organization follow the correct sequence and pass through the right manufacturing processes before being converted into the finished products. Transportation department used to take over the responsibility of finished products or materials from PPC as soon as these were produced and packed and distribute the same to the right place at the right time. Transportation which was a part of logistics used to be handled by sales/marketing people, who were taking care of distribution of products also at the same time.

In some organizations, materials management function also was introduced. Classic materials management includes the function of forecasting, inventory management, stores management, warehousing, stock keeping, and scheduling till it came to include production planning and control to evolve into extended materials management (Chopra *et al.*, 2007). This ensured that a single entity was responsible for the management of entire movement of materials right from the supplier end to warehousing. This helped the organization avoid the cost of noncooperation and minimal information sharing among entities involved in the process. Responsibility of transporting, warehousing, and distribution of the materials was vested on the marketing department, who gave always higher priority to marketing activities and meet the sales target rather than concentrating on body of knowledge available for logistics and distribution functions. Council of supply chain management professional (CSCMP) defined logistics and distribution "as that part of the supply chain management which plans, implements, and controls the efficient, effective, forward, and reverse flow and storage of goods, services, and related information between the point of origin and point of consumption in order to meet customers' requirements" vide their website (*cscmp.org* accessed on 4th December, 2013). Thus, a supply chain encompassed the operations starting from vendors' vendors to customers' customers.

*****

Chapter III
Motivation

Presently businesses are expanding into international markets and requirement of today is to manage the business and distribution across the globe apart from the traditional requirement of *highest quality at lowest cost.* Cross company concepts, referred to as supply chain management are necessary to meet these increasing demands (Krikke *et al.,* 2003). Over the past decade, the traditional purchasing and logistics functions have evolved into a broader strategic approach to materials and distribution management known as supply chain management (Tan, 2001). Time has arrived when individual efficiency is replaced by team efficiency and that is where the success of SCM lies. Based on the experience and real-life experiences in industries, following main factors were found to be the real motivators for organizations in adopting the concept and survive in a fiercely competitive global market.

- Quantum jump of Information technology (internet, e-mail, e-procurement, B to B exchange and various analytical tools)
- Customer and peer pressure
- Complexities associated with globalization of operations/sourcing
- Awareness of Japanese Culture/systems (suppliers are partners in progress)
- Benefits of innovative production and quality systems (ISO 9000, TS 16949, TPM, TQM and SIX-SIGMA)
- Availability of sophisticated production and process technology at reasonable cost (CNC machines).

- Availability of skilled and educated workforce
- Recognition of potential benefit of information sharing and cross functional integration
- Liberal economic policies of the governments of developing countries.

Since the materials constitute almost 60% of the cost of manufactured products with possible exceptions of some electronic goods incorporating innovative frontier technologies (Fuller *et al.*, 1993) management of the entire chain of supplies became important and probably only tool to reduce the cost of the supply chain to improve the bottom line and at the same time satisfy service level requirement of customers. According to the council of logistics management (CLM) supply chain management could be defined as the integration of key business   processes from supplier end to customer end which add value for the customers and others who have a stake in the organization? Simchi-Levi *et al.* (2003) defined SCM as "a set of approaches utilized to efficiently integrate suppliers, manufacturers, warehouses and stores so that merchandise is produced and distributed at the right quantities, to the right locations, and at the right time in order to minimize system wide costs while satisfying service level requirements". To be precise SCM is an outgrowth of pair of previous perspectives, the upstream focused procurement of supply management orientation of the manufacturer and supplier and the downstream focused transportation and logistics perspective of the distributor and retailer (Tan, 2001). Because it is fairly a new concept there are a variety of models with no standard definition having yet emerged (Tan, 2001 and Gibson *et. al.,* 2005,). According to Chopra et al. (2010), SCM has thus emerged as an integrative philosophy and strategic level business practices which encompasses flow of materials, funds and information throughout the network that ultimately delivers value to the customer. The supply chain operation reference model (SCOR) spans entire supply chain from supplier's supplier to customer's customer. SCM to be precise should thus encompass suppliers' suppliers to customers' customers by integrating and managing all the processes involved in the entire system through proper information sharing, mutual trust, use of appropriate technology and expertise, joint development and benefit sharing. Organizations have started adopting SCM practices, which could be called as the management of chain of supplies, in true spirit right from nineties across the globe. In the context of SCM, logistics also included flow of materials into the organizations (inbound) apart from flow of the same from the organizations (outbound) and intra-company flow of materials (manufacturing). The objective of the supply chain should be to maximize the overall value generated. The value (also known as supply chain surplus) a supply chain generates is the difference between what the final product is worth to the customer and costs the supply chain incurs in satisfying the customers. A supply chain consists of all parties involved directly or indirectly in fulfilling customer requirements (Chopra and Meindl, 2007).

****

Chapter IV
Definition and Structure

A typical supply chain, which may involve a variety of stages, is an integrated process wherein a number of business entities (suppliers, manufacturers, distributors and retailers) work together in an effort to acquire raw materials, convert these raw materials into final products and deliver these products to final customers.

Raw materials are procured from the supplier, transformed into finished products in manufacturing, and then transported to the retailers through distributors and finally delivered to the end customer and this supply chain is also termed as a value chain many a time. Supply chain exists in all kinds of industries such as electronic goods, pharmaceuticals, garments, food products, and service organizations.

Complexity and structure of the supply chain vary based on the type of industry. Supply chains exist in both service and manufacturing organizations, although the complexity of the chain may vary significantly from industry to industry and firm to firm. A supply chain comprises of different functional level. Each functional level consists of an echelon and there may be numerous facilities within the echelon. Along with the functional level and various facilities in each echelon, flow of information also contributes to the complex supply chain structure (Shah, 2009). This complexity has led to the structural classification based on material and information flow. Supply chain can be classified into different structures such as serial, convergent, divergent, conjoint and general structures (Beamon and Chen, 2001). In the serial structure, the product goes through a series of production/assembly stages as in mass production or continuous manufacturing. Where a series of assembly operations are carried out to obtain the final product the supply chain structure is called a *convergent* one. Examples include aircrafts, construction industry, etc. Similarly, if customization starts in early production phases and a wide variety of finished products are produced with a limited number of raw materials or components it is called a *divergent* supply chain. Examples of such supply chains include electro-mechanical systems such as motors; textiles; metal fabrications; and chemicals. There may be another one named conjoined one where it is a combination of convergent and divergent supply chains.

49

However, the schematic representation of serial supply chain is what is presented in Figure. 4.1.

Flow of materials and information

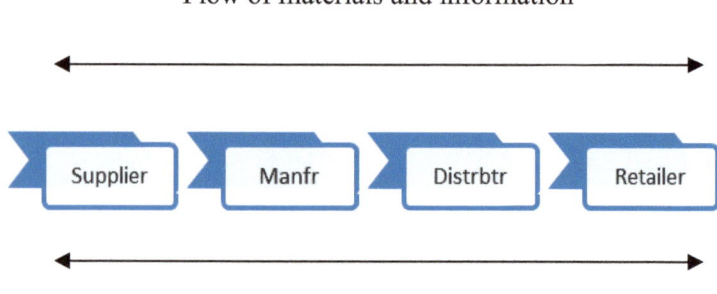

Flow of money and information

Figure 4.1 Schematic representation of forward supply chain

Optimizing the supply chain networks in the real-world business environment is a very difficult task because the supply chain leader, usually referred to the manufacturer along the supply chain, has to deal with uncertainties in supply and demand with conflicting objectives and tradeoffs among the different elements along the chain (Kannan *et. al.*, 2010). Since all the activities take place in the forward direction from suppliers' suppliers to customers' customers in sequence i.e. from left to right the chain is what is called forward supply chain. A typical supply chain is shown in Figure 4.2.

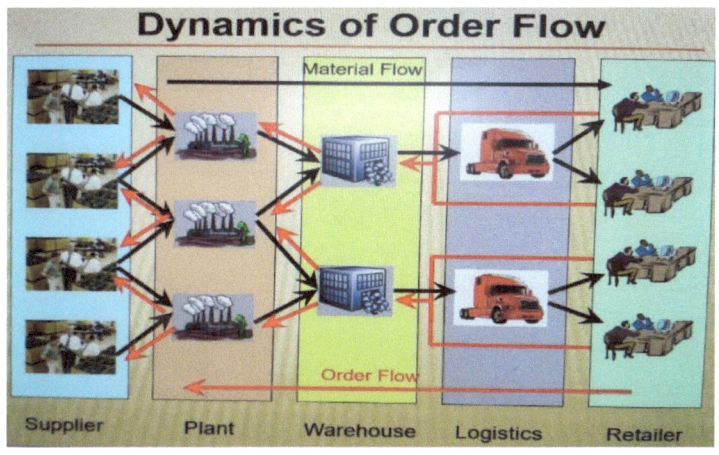

Figure 4.2 A typical supply chain of an industrial product

****

Chapter V
Way Forward

Productivity in Forward supply chain could be increased by reducing the cost of labor and material. Until recently the focus was on the labor input with the introduction of advanced systems, sophisticated equipment and latest management techniques, which resulted in productivity going up by three hundred percent during the last fifty years (Turner, 2012). Material productivity remained untapped for quite some time till it was felt that mother earth's capacity of supplying fossil fuel and other raw materials is not infinite and the area on the surface of the mother earth for dumping wastes is dwindling. Society was also worried that increase in output gradually vitiated the environment and affected the health of the people apart from other living animals, birds etc. Hence what is the solution to overcome the problem? Aiming for *zero waste* seems to be only solution available. Customers' pressure on one side to reduce the cost still further and the pressure of regulatory authority and outcry of the society on the other side for cleaner environment compelled the manufacturers to rethink of reusing parts/products especially for recycling of costly raw materials. This process of recovering raw materials and products is likely to improve the efficiency of supply chain to a great extent without disturbing the ecosystem of our earth. In fact, researchers have neglected the area of remanufacturing till early nineties although *going the wrong way* or the movement of products back from the customers for remanufacturing have been going on for centuries typically for high value and low volume items like locomotive

engines and aircrafts (Guide *et al.*, 2008).

Supply chain management has done a lot in terms of customer satisfaction and cost reduction, but with shelf life of products narrowing down there is huge generation of scrap, which if managed properly can further improve the efficiency of the supply chain. Although researchers were constantly working on the various aspects of forward movement of materials in FSC right from early nineties to understand its efficacy as well as the impact of it however the movement of materials upstream from the customers/consumers backward has not received much attention (Simchi *et. al* 2003). Academics dismissed this as insignificant. Question is – 'Is the management ready to consider the returns management or reverse supply chain (RSC) as a business proposition like FSC or treat this as a dirty job?

Presentation was over and everybody seems to be perturbed probably thinking that this would be the time when the Chairman would probably ask us to come out of the silos and collaborate with each other.

"It was an impressive lecture but it seems we are to learn a lot from Mr. Bhattacharya. This is just the tip of the iceberg. Robin, when are we coming for a presentation on Reverse supply chain and then on to closed loop supply chain?"

"Next month, Sir, I would be ready with Reverse Supply chain presentation."

"All right, fix up a date and inform me I would be present if it is held during the first week."

Chairman left the room.

"Robin, why are you bringing all the new things every time? We are comfortable now and do not want to be out of the comfort zone" Charles said.

"If you cannot change the ways you are doing things now you cannot change the results you are expecting." I replied.

"You are really crazy" saying this Charles, our General Manager Operations, left in a huff.

Journey has just begun! I came out of the meeting hall and looked at the sky. It was a full moon night and I drenched myself in the cool shower of the moon rays. The gentle breeze flowed past me and I enjoyed every moment of this. I felt rejuvenated for my next presentation!

****

REFERENCES

Beamon, B.M. and V.C.P. Chen (2001). Performance analysis of conjoined supply chains. *International Journal of Production Research,* 39(14), *3195-3218.*

Chan, F. T., and Qi, H. J. (2003). An innovative performance measurement method for supply chain management. *Supply Chain Management: An International Journal*, 8(3), 209-223.

Chopra, Sunil and Peter Meindl. (2007), Supply Chain Management: Strategy, Planning, and Operation.

Corsten, D., and Kumar, N. (2005). Do suppliers benefit from collaborative relationships with large retailers? An empirical investigation of efficient consumer response adoption. *Journal of Marketing*, 69 (3), 80-94.

Dudek, G., and Stadtler, H. (2005). Negotiation-based collaborative planning between supply chains partners. *European Journal of Operational Research*,163(3), 668-687.

Dong, Y., and Xu, K. (2002). A supply chain model of vendor managed inventory. *Transportation Research*

Part E: Logistics and Transportation Review, *38*(2), 75-95.

Fuller, J., O'Conor, J. and R. Rawlinson. (1993). Tailored logistics: the next advantage, *Harvard Business Review*, 71(3), 87-98.

Gibson, B. J., Mentzer, J. T., and Cook, R. L. (2005) Supply chain management: the pursuit of a consensus definition. *Journal of Business Logistics*, 26(2), 17-25.

Guide, V. D. R. Jr., Wassenhove, V. L. N. (2008) *The Evolution of Closed-Loop Supply Chain Research.* Working Papers collection, 7, 1 – 34, INSEAD, France.

Krikke, H. (2003). Impact of closed-loop network configurations on carbon footprints: A case study in copiers, *Resources, conservation and recycling, 55*(12), 1196-1205.

Lamming, R. (2005) Supplier relationship management. In *Perspektiven des supply management* (pp. 81-94). Springer Berlin Heidelberg.

Lummus R, Duclos LK, and Vokurka RJ. (2003) Supply chain flexibility: building a new model. *Glob J Flex Syst Manage*, 4(4),1–13

Spieler, A. C. and Murray, A. S. (2008). Management Controlled Firms v. Owner Controlled Firms: A Historical Perspective of Ownership Concentration in the US, East

East Asia and the EU. *J. Int'l Bus. & L.*, *7*, 49.

Simchi-Levi, D., & Zhao, Y. (2003) The value of information sharing in a two-stage supply chain with production capacity constraints. Naval Research Logistics (NRL), 50(8), 888-916.

Tan, K. C. (2001) A framework of supply chain management literature. *European Journal of Purchasing & Supply Management*, *7*(1), 39-48.

****